HAROLD KLEMP

THE
AWAKENED
HEART

HAROLD KLEMP

ECKANKAR
Minneapolis
www.Eckankar.org

ABOUT THIS BOOK: *The Awakened Heart* is compiled from Harold Klemp's writings. These selections originally appeared in his books published by Eckankar.

The Awakened Heart

060903

Printed in USA
Compiled by John Kulick
Edited by Patrick Carroll, Joan Klemp, and Anthony Moore
Cover photo: Jim Brandenburg/Minden Pictures
Text photo by Robert Huntley
Cover design by Doug Munson

Library of Congress Cataloging-in-Publication Data
Klemp, Harold.
   [Selections. 2007]
   The awakened heart / Harold Klemp ; [compiled by John Kulick].
      p. cm.
   ISBN-13: 978-1-57043-246-0 (hardcover : alk. paper)
 I. Eckankar (Organization) 2. Love—Religious aspects.
 I. Kulick, John. II. Title.
   BP605.E3K546 2007
   299'.93—dc22
                                        2007012775

∞ This paper meets the requirements of ANSI/NISO Z39.48-1992 (Permanence of Paper).

Contents

v

DEAR READER

How can we fill ourselves with the blessings of God? The answers are contained in this extraordinary book, the fifth volume in Harold Klemp's award-winning Immortality of Soul series.

In *The Awakened Heart,* author Harold Klemp shows us how to graciously and gracefully live our life from a higher state of consciousness as a Co-worker with God.

Every page holds a key to help us on our journey. You can read one quote each day and contemplate its meaning. Take your time and remember that God's love comes from the inside out.

God's truth is written in your heart.

GRACEFUL LIVING

Graceful living, being gracious, means that you are filled with the blessings of God. And if you are filled with the blessings of God, you will certainly be someone who lives gracefully and graciously with others.

All in all, earth is still nothing more than a spiritual school. It was set up and designed by God so that each one of you, each Soul in this world, can learn more about becoming godlike.

This is the whole purpose of why you are here: to become more godlike.

*S*oul is the true being that you are. You are Soul.

*B*uild. Act in an uplifting man-
ner, and the Law of Life will never repay
you in a negative way.

*W*hat can you do to become more spiritual?

A very simple spiritual exercise is to sing the word *HU* (pronounced like *hue*), as a love song to God.

When you sing HU, you are opening your heart to the love and protection of God.

You also open yourself to wisdom, insight, compassion, and many other divine qualities.

If you are into physical fitness, you run, walk, ride a bicycle, or find some kind of exercise that will keep you fit.

There are also exercises that keep us fit spiritually.

The spiritual exercises open your heart to the Light and Sound of God, which is simply divine love, the love of God. When your heart opens to love, with it come wisdom and understanding.

*P*eople who sing HU, the most beautiful prayer, open themselves to the Light and Sound of God, which is divine love.

*T*he Sound and Light of God are the appearance of God's love in your daily life in a very real way. Sometimes you'll feel a vibration, sometimes you might hear the music of a flute. These are both manifestations of the Sound of God.

People see the Light of God inwardly as a white light, a blue light, a pink light, a green light, sometimes in the form of a lightbulb, sometimes as a fire, sometimes as a lamp, or just as a globe that glows—It can be any form, any color.

The highest truth is not written in any book, it's written in your heart. All the books in the world are useless unless they can help you open your heart.

Open your heart to what? To the love of God.

*L*ove is like water in that only so much can be poured into the glass. Before you can put more in, you have to let some out. If you don't keep giving out love, more can't come in.

People often wonder, *How do I get God's love?* You get it by giving of yourself to others, in ways that you like to give.

When you are with others, realize that they too are lights of God who are also trying to find their way home to a better, happier, more graceful life.

TO GIVE
IS TO LIVE

*I*f you love, then all things will come to you. At some point love will begin to direct all your actions and thoughts. Then you can accept life.

As we give of ourselves, of our patience and love, to someone who needs it, something changes inside us. Something flows in, a flow of good feeling.

A spiritual upliftment occurs both in us and in the person receiving the love.

*A*s a gift of love is given, it must be returned.

$\mathcal{Y}$ou find you get a great deal of love from just looking after the well-being of those Souls who look to you for some of their spiritual food.

*W*e look for the divine nature that exists in other people as well as in ourselves.

*I*deas suddenly come to us on how to make our work easier or make something work out better for someone else.

Where do these ideas come from? From the creative imagination, the godlike part of us. This is God in expression.

*S*ometimes you are called upon by the ECK, the Holy Spirit, to go out of your way to help another person toward the enlightenment of God.

*I*f your inner life changes to where you have no experience of the Sound or Light of God, this is very natural when you understand the cycles of life.

The quiet period is a time of rest. But it's also a time where you learn to give back to life what you have received inwardly through the Holy Spirit.

The spiritual principle is you get the most effect out of everything you do, then everything is turned to a spiritual effect.

Everything in our life, all the forces, instead of being scattered all over and being wasteful, are aligned through the spiritual exercises in one direction. That direction is toward God.

Self-responsibility is the key to spiritual freedom.

Develop the creative side of yourself so you can figure out your own problems. The creative power works best through those who love what they are doing.

To give is to live, and this is why I talk about service. If you want to live more spiritually, then you must give more and more in the way of service to all life.

CONTEMPLATION IS APPRECIATION

---

*A*nother word for contemplation is *appreciation*. Think about all the reasons you have to be grateful.

Think about the gifts in your life that have come from God, from the Holy Spirit, that make this life worth living. Think about the adventures that are coming, and be grateful for the strength to meet tomorrow.

*I*n contemplation you simply sit and quietly sing HU or some other holy name of God, allowing the Voice of God to come into you, either as love or as Light or Sound.

All you need do to recognize and benefit from these gifts of the Holy Spirit is to open your consciousness.

We open the consciousness through the Spiritual Exercises of ECK, such as singing HU.

*T*he ECK, or Holy Spirit, uses any number of ways to bring you answers or insights about the right thing to do.

It brings confirmation into your life in times of doubt.

*W*ithout the protection of divine love, even the most idle thought creates a karmic situation that needs to be resolved sometime later.

We learn to protect ourselves by singing HU.

If you have one of these thoughts and you're aware of it, just say, "Whoops, I really don't need that experience," and sing HU.

You never know when the Holy Spirit may tap you on the shoulder and ask you to be a channel for It. These experiences come often to the person who does the spiritual exercises and keeps his heart open.

*Y*ou serve God by being open to the Holy Spirit and going about your life. And if someone needs help, you help where you can.

The quickest way to put your state of consciousness in the heart of God is to sing HU. Just sing HU-U-U-U to yourself a few times. You'll notice that something changes.

*T*he person you are now is entirely different from the child you were years ago. You're not the same person anymore, because you have a different consciousness today.

*Y*our consciousness is expanding outwardly in concentric circles, reaching further and further to encompass the knowledge needed to make better decisions—the knowledge to run your life better.

*T*rue contemplation is reflecting on the blessings of God in your life. It's not complex, there are many ways to do it, and it certainly will enrich you.

IF GOD CAME DOWN

*I*f you would consider that you are Soul, a child of God, you could then consider that every other person is also a child of God.

Christ spoke about this when he said to love your neighbor as yourself. You must first of all learn to love yourself. To love yourself means to love your divine qualities—compassion, goodness, and love.

You cannot comprehend more than your experience in life has given you the capacity to understand. Therefore, you must recognize that while your understanding of God is sacred, so also is your neighbor's.

*I*f there is a crime, it's growing old too fast. It's becoming so sure of ourselves.

When that happens, we've stopped listening to the Voice of God, which is the Holy Spirit. The Voice of God is speaking to us every day, in every way, in the smallest things in our everyday lives.

A family consists of people learning to become more spiritual by being with others. One thing you learn is that you can't have everything your own way.

*M*y job is simply to make you aware that there is such a thing as the Light and Sound of God and then help you become aware of your own divinity.

*I*f you can achieve peace of mind and a state of joy when all those around you are losing theirs, you have come much further than many people today.

*Y*ou may see chaos and destruction around you and know that there will never be a heaven on earth. But you can have heaven on earth within your own heart.

*R*emember that our goal is to become a Co-worker with God. This means we become fully able to help in the divine plan of serving life.

*U*ntil you can take care of yourself, you cannot take care of anyone else.
This is the principle behind a Co-worker
with God.

The HU is a very real, spiritual vitamin. It is a holy name of God which will lift you into the higher worlds.

You are a child of God. If you have forgotten, you might try singing HU, the love song to God.

But remember to sing it with your whole heart. Otherwise, you'll never find the blessings of God.

TEST OF GRACE

$\mathcal{O}$ne of the most important things we need to learn is how to be gracious and graceful in our everyday life.

*M*any parts of the world are facing hard times now. As quickly as things ease off in one part of the world, they become harder in another; that's the nature of this schoolroom of God.

Earth is a schoolroom where each of you can become aware of the purpose of this existence, which is to become a more spiritual being. It's to help you become a better Co-worker with God.

*E*ach of us is Soul, and we are here to learn lessons. One of the great lessons is to learn to love yourself. Until you can do that, you cannot learn to love someone else.

And until you can learn to love yourself and others, you cannot truly love God.

Loving ourselves is hard for many of us because we know ourselves so well. But it's a necessary step, and we have to do the best we can.

When you are having the hardest time, you are probably unfolding the most. This is because life in the lower worlds needs a balance.

*T*he difference between you and another person isn't that you're better, it's that you understand your purpose better. But even that is nothing unless you do something about it and live what you know. This is important.

The highest principle you can live is divine love. This is living in the spirit of God's love.

*R*ealize that as you give love to God, God's love has already been given to you. Now all you need do is accept God's love and return it to life.

For in returning it to life, to your fellow man and other creatures of God, you are returning it to God.

*S*piritual law requires that you go either forward or backward.

This is a fact of life, a spiritual principle. You must unfold, or you shrink spiritually. Things move forward or backward.

*W*ithout humility, all forward progress on the path to God is stopped.

*P*art of the process of unfolding spiritually is to learn what makes your life more interesting and better, and also the things to stay away from.

We do not expect a vacation for eternity after this life is over. What we expect is a steady progression in spiritual unfoldment from this life to the next life, and on and on.

We are here on earth to learn love and compassion, to become a more perfect spiritual being.

THE DIFFERENT LEVELS OF DREAMS

*I*n a sense, this life is a dream. If the so-called dreams we have are figments of the imagination, then so is this life.

But on the other hand if this life is real, then perhaps there is more reality to the dream life than we have been able to recognize or accept in the past.

*T*here are four levels of dreams in daily life. Although we consider daily life not to be a dream, I'm saying that it, too, is part of the dream of God.

First there are the images or pictures, such as on the TV news, that are part of our everyday reality.

*T*he second level of dreams is waking dreams. This is when a spiritual influence comes into an individual's life from the other side. An angel speaks to someone, protects someone, heals someone; there is prophecy or a visit from an ECK Master.

A waking dream brings an influence and makes a connection for that person with some outer event. Basically there is something supernatural taking place, a spiritual intervention. It will affect the behavior of the individual toward good, toward spiritual growth.

*T*he third level is sleeping dreams. Here again there's a connection between the inner worlds which are real and this outer world. People who study dreams can become very adept at seeing how to take care of their own health, what's coming in the immediate or distant future, how to deal with relationships both at home and at work, and things of this nature.

Dreams can help you analyze your own situation and help you live a better life.

*T*he fourth level is actually beyond the dream level, and it is the experiences that come in contemplation. Or in meditation for those of you who meditate.

Our purpose in studying dreams is to make you a better spiritual being. Dreams can help you in your goal of becoming a Co-worker with God.

*I*f you understand dreams and how they work, you can use your dreams to take the next step in your own life.

An effective way is to use dreams together with the Spiritual Exercises of ECK. A simple one is to sing HU at bedtime for five or ten minutes before you go to sleep. It spiritualizes your state of consciousness.

Forget about your intent to have any kind of special dream. Just fill your heart with love, and go to sleep. Do this nightly, and soon you will find your dreams provide a key for a happier, more spiritual life.

*D*reams can help you in your daily life. They can help you see what's coming. They can help you see why things are as they are.

You'll find you were a key player in the circumstances that brought the situations you find yourself in today.

*I*f you can get into the habit of writing down your dreams, the full spectrum of your life will open to you slowly and gradually, the way the petals of a flower open.

*D*reams can sometimes foretell the future.

The ECK-Vidya, the ancient science of prophecy, is for special occasions when at a certain important crossroads in life, you need extra help, love, or support. This is when your dreams may bring a message that gives you comfort, strength, insight, patience, compassion, or whatever you need.

*D*reams are a doorway to other aspects of Soul in Its natural state.

Soul has the ability to move back and forth from the physical world to higher planes, and It can learn to do this at will. Beginning in the dream state It can move into a higher, more alert, more aware state of consciousness we call Soul Travel.

Soul Travel is simply opening your heart to God's love and being able to ride on that wave.

When a spiritual experience comes into our daily life, we're often too involved in it to see the message. If it had been handed to us in a dream, the significance would have been as clear as a bell.

LIVING IN THE MOMENT

*T*here is a step beyond prophecy. This is the ability to live in the moment.

*T*he future comes up on us unseen. It is for this reason we must concern our-selves with *now*; to live in the moment.

Be aware that you are alive, that you are gaining experience.

*T*he true spiritual path is always working for the betterment of you and everyone around you.

One of the ways the ECK, or Holy Spirit, gives direction to the individual is through the Golden-tongued Wisdom.

It gives us a deep insight into the present and also lets us look at the past. It makes something appear in a golden light or jump out of context at us: something the Holy Spirit calls to our attention in our daily life for our own good.

What we are trying to achieve is the upliftment of spiritual consciousness through our creative abilities.

*D*ivine Spirit will help you in the direction you need for your unfoldment.

But when things do go wrong, as they will, don't say, "God has forsaken me." Rather say, "God loves me so much that He's giving me the opportunity to learn this about myself, to learn how to become a more spiritual being."

$\mathcal{S}$elf-mastery simply means a person has the ability to run his own life according to the laws of Spirit.

This presumes you know the laws of Spirit. The understanding of these laws comes through the Light and Sound of God.

*S*oul is a unique being, which means there is only one of you at a time in any of the universes of God. Your personal experiences set you apart.

To become a conscious vehicle for God requires that you become the very best you can possibly be in whatever you choose to do.

*L*ife and death really have no borders; it's all part of the continuum of life. We learn how to operate, live, and have our being in the continuum of life.

I learned a long time ago to be a humble servant for the Holy Spirit and let it be at that.

Love life, do what you can to get along peacefully with others, defend yourself when necessary, and give compassion when you can. And go on through life.

GOD'S LOVE COMES FROM THE INSIDE OUT

---

*D*ivine Spirit uses small examples
in your life to teach you about divine love.
It does this by putting your opinion on the
line—whenever you have strong feelings
about something.

We are most aware of Soul in the human form, so people in their limited state of awareness and understanding of spiritual knowledge generally say, "We have a soul, people have a soul."

As I've said, we *are* Soul and as Soul we *have* a body—an important distinction.

*G*od's love extends equally to all crea-tures—human, animal, vegetable, mineral. If a person understands this, then that person has the beginning of wisdom.

*H*ow do we treat God's creatures? How do we treat other people? How do we treat ourselves? How do we act? How do we think?

The law of life known as the Law of Karma is the great teacher. As you sow, so shall ye reap. It's not a vindictive law; it's a law designed to open the heart to love and understanding.

*D*ivine love comes to us in surprising ways, often unrecognized ways. So that when it does come, we do not recognize that the Holy Spirit has spoken to us—to help make our sojourn in this world a little better, a little more enlightening.

*N*obody else can carry us to heaven. Nobody else can help us be what we won't be ourselves.

*T*hrough the Spiritual Exercises of ECK—as you create an open door for yourself into a greater world—you'll get into the habit of looking for a brighter, more creative world out here.

If someone were to ask me, "You have different aspects to your teachings, like dreams, Soul Travel, the ECK-Vidya (knowing the future), healing, and all these different things. What would you call the most important?"

Without doubt and without question I would say, "It's love, divine love."

*E*verything in life depends on love.
God is love, and creation exists because God
loves it. Creation exists because of Souls—
billions of Souls at different levels of awareness.

*L*ove is a graceful thing. Love is always sharing, telling people who need to know about God's love in a way they can understand.

*T*here is no way that I, any other person, or any physical book of scriptures—no matter how holy—can open your heart. And whether people know it or not, believe it or not, the heart opens from the inside out.

God's love comes from the inside out.

GAINING A HIGHER STATE OF CONSCIOUSNESS

*W*hat are the signs of people who have high spiritual consciousness?

Whenever you see someone acting with love, goodwill, charity, compassion, and qualities of this nature—a person who actually lives these qualities—you're seeing a genuine person.

Then you can say, "This is someone living in the Light and Sound of God."

There are those who know divine love. It doesn't matter whether they're in Eckankar or any of the many other religions. It doesn't matter. They may not belong to any religion at all.

But from experiences in past lives some people understand the quality of divine love. And these people recognize each other when they meet.

*T*here is no absolute way to regard the highest spiritual unfoldment, because those who have gone into the higher levels of consciousness realize there is always one more step to unfoldment.

*S*ometimes being a channel for God requires simply that you be aware in a situation where someone is in pain, in sorrow, or in a state of loneliness or heartbreak.

You just listen. If you are just listening, sometimes people can speak.

*F*ear is what separates Soul from God's love.

If you can work through this self-made barrier of fear that's within you, you will find a greater degree of divine love. And this will stay with you.

*S*omething I appreciate more than anything in everyday life is finding a person through whom the Light of God is shining. Some people have an attitude that says, "I like your company. We have business to do, but we might as well enjoy doing business."

People who have this attitude are open-hearted. They love their work. And through this love for their work, they are reflecting the love of God.

*T*he imagination is the God-spark within you. The only gift of God we can rightly lay claim to in the physical body is the gift of imagination.

If you learn how to use the full powers of the imagination and direct them toward the spiritual exercises, you will be able to find ways around the blocks set up by the mind.

Trust in Spirit to bring you whatever you need for your unfoldment.

Who and what you are doesn't concern me. All that concerns me is that the Soul willing to make Its way back home to God has every opportunity to do so.

All I am offering you is a glimpse
of the face of God through personal experiences in the Light and Sound of this Divine
Being.

We are looking to achieve the kingdom of heaven, which means the state of high awareness or God Consciousness, while in the physical body.

ONE STEP AWAY

---

*S*oul can create whatever It needs.

transition from the old to the new happens gradually, in stages.

Sometimes God or a better life is so close, so close. But many people choose to stay on one side of the wall simply because they cannot recognize that a better life is right there on the other side.

Change means going from one state of consciousness to another. And this involves adjustments, which in most cases mean trouble. Adjustments equal trouble.

But when you get to the other side, all of a sudden you realize that things are better. That this life, this state, this new condition existed alongside the original one all along.

A person's state of consciousness makes him happy or unhappy.

It's what you do with what you have that makes all the difference. Whenever something comes into my life, I try to get the most out of it I can.

The Holy Spirit, which is the Voice of God, is always working on your behalf to help you unfold spiritually, to become a better, more loving human being.

All that prevents you from taking that step is your state of awareness, your focus on God. How strong is it? How much do you want God?

How successful you will be depends on your answer.

*T*here's no hurry in the spiritual life. You don't go after God in the same way that you go after a promotion in the office. It's much different.

*L*ike an early spring flower, some people unfold sooner than others. Why? It's the individuality of Soul, the difference between each of us. Soul picks Its own path to God, in Its own time, in Its own way.

When we work from the Soul consciousness, we can shape our own destiny.

*S*ome people think visualization is an empty fantasy, but it's not. We couldn't imagine something unless there was a reality to it.

You do what you can to make your life right, and when you have done 100 percent of everything you can do, then Spirit steps in to help with the miracle.

LETTING GO OF YOUR FEAR

*D*ivine love begins first with yourself. Until you learn to love yourself, you cannot love someone else.

Until you learn to love yourself, you cannot even love God.

*W*here love exists there can be no fear; and where there is fear, there can be no truth.

When fear is a dominant force in your life, it takes away the joy and freedom of living.

*P*eople who are afraid to get on with life are actually afraid of death.

When you gain power over the fear of death, there is nothing that can hold you back in this life.

*G*uilt and fear stand between us and
our true spiritual heritage.

*T*he best spiritual opportunity is not necessarily the easiest life.

Sometimes the best way to learn the spiritual lessons is through a life of hardship.

*B*eing relaxed in the arms of ECK means giving up and letting go of your fear to Divine Spirit. Because that is the ECK, the Holy Spirit.

If you're going to be a Co-worker with God, you need to be strong.

*T*here is a way to bring peace and harmony to yourself even in the most difficult of times.

*T*oday there is greater need to tell people about ECK, the teachings of the Holy Spirit.

The teachings show people how to find love, wisdom, and spiritual freedom. And to find this within themselves, within their hearts.

*O*nce ignorance and fear are removed from our lives, we enter into the freedom of Soul. We can then come into the states of wisdom, power, and freedom.

THE AWAKENED HEART

*F*ear keeps us from living life to the fullest. And until we can live life to the fullest, we cannot know the meaning of the awakened heart.

*M*ost of the things we fear never happen to us, while the things we never considered do happen. Life always catches us looking in the wrong direction. It blindsides us.

There are so many different lessons that life presents in order to teach us about the fullness of God's love.

There is a bond between the various religions, and that bond is love for God. The difference comes in the understanding of God. It is as different between religions as it is between the members of any one religion or even any one church.

What causes this disparity? The difference is in how much of God's love each of us can accept. And how much we can accept depends upon our life experiences.

*I*t doesn't matter what religion you are in; it doesn't make a bit of difference. The only thing that matters is love for God, and that means letting other people be. Give them the freedom that you want for yourself. Love your neighbor as yourself.

This is the message Christ was trying to convey. If it really were understood by those who proclaim God's love, we would see an entirely different world.

*L*ove also comes through to some people in the form of a healing. Unless you have the consciousness to see what is taking place, you will totally miss the love of God coming into your life.

*T*he love of God has no strings at-
tached. Yet, the love of God demands total
responsibility to God for our actions.

*M*any lessons come through the gift of love. Divine love comes through human love. They really are the same, except that human love is an imperfect expression of divine love.

*N*o two people have the same understanding of God's love. Whereas one may speak of divine love, another lives it.

Most people who live divine love speak about it very little.

When love fills our heart, it becomes the awakened heart.

We suddenly see and understand all there is to know about life itself—that it is good, that it is necessary, and that we exist because God loves us. That's all there is to the mystery of life. Soul exists because God loves It.

ABOUT THE AUTHOR

Author Harold Klemp is known as a pioneer of today's focus on "everyday spirituality." He was raised on a Wisconsin farm and attended divinity school. He also served in the U.S. Air Force.

In 1981, after years of training, he became the spiritual leader of Eckankar, Religion of the Light and Sound of God. His mission is to help people find their way back to God in this life.

Harold Klemp speaks each year to thousands of seekers at Eckankar seminars. Author of more than sixty books, he continues to write, including many articles and spiritual-study discourses. Harold Klemp's inspiring and practical approach to spirituality helps thousands of people worldwide find greater freedom, wisdom, and love in their lives.